QURAN COMPANION

A Memorization Journal

PROJECT LED BY:

Mufti Sayyid Abdul Samad al-Qadiri

THIS BOOK IS DEDICATED TO:

HAFIZ AL-MILLAH
SHAYKH ABD AL-AZIZ MURADABADI

QURAN COMPANION: A MEMORIZATION GUIDE
COPYRIGHT Ⓒ 2025 THESUNNIWAY

CONTACT@THESUNNIWAY.COM

ISBN: 978-1-957773-66-7

يقال لصاحب القرآن اقرأ وارتق ورتل كما كنت
ترتل في الدنيا فإن منزلك عند آخر آية تقرؤها

It will be said to the companion of the Qur'ān, "Recite and ascend! And recite in
a measured tone as you would recite in a measured tone in the temporary world,
for indeed, your station is at the last verse you recite!"

SUNAN 'ABŪ DĀWŪD

STUDENT NAME

TABLE OF CONTENTS

TABLE OF CONTENTS

TABLE OF CONTENTS

TABLE OF CONTENTS

TABLE OF CONTENTS

TABLE OF CONTENTS

INTRODUCTION

الحمد لله وحده والصلوة والسلام على من لا نبي بعده

The word for word, letter for letter, preservation of the Noble Qur'ān is an asset which the faithful take great pride in. The credit of this bounty belongs solely to Allāh Almighty, as it is He who has provided this exclusivity to the Muslims by preserving His book Himself. Allāh Almighty states:

إِنَّا نَحْنُ نَزَّلْنَا ٱلذِّكْرَ وَإِنَّا لَهُۥ لَحَٰفِظُونَ

"Indeed, We have revealed the remembrance, and We, for it, are protectors."
(al-Ḥijr:9)

The manner in which Allāh Almighty has preserved His word is remarkable to say the least. It is a book memorized even by children who are yet to learn how to read. Whenever a mistake is committed in the recitation of its words, be it in the midst of ṣalāh where a believer silently heeds the words of Allāh, anyone who knows the sūrah being recited calls out with a correction. This is the degree to which this book is preserved. To play any role, as insignificant as the role may seem, in the preservation of the Noble Qur'ān is an honor provided by Allāh Almighty, and all men and women of faith should strive to commit at least a portion, in accordance with their ability, of His miraculous word to memory with this purpose of contributing to the preservation of His book.

The Noble Qur'ān should be recited, memorized, learned, understood, and reflected on. Any relation with the book of Allāh is a means of reward, but its memorization is generally seen to be the most difficult task, and it is due to this that upon reaching adulthood, many retire its memorization and seek to suffice the remainder of their lives with that which they have memorized when their minds were sharper. This is a communal issue which requires remedy. Memorization of the Qur'ān is not a task exclusive to children or to those who have dedicated the majority of their day for its cause. Rather, the memorization and recitation should be a lifelong journey, and it should be kept in mind that although the memorization may become more difficult with growing age, that is no excuse to live one's life only having memorized a few sūrahs of the end. What one receives of his results in memorization is proportionate to his efforts and the blessings of Allāh Almighty upon him.

To memorize from the Qur'ān, one should exert sincere efforts, and to enhance the fruits of his efforts, one may find great benefit in assigning himself a companion for his memorization. The tradition of memorizing and reciting the Qur'ān with a companion is an age-old practice which finds its roots in the blessed era of the Noble Prophet, upon him be blessings and salutations, and even Sayyidunā Jibrīl, upon him be salutations, would recite the Qur'ān to the Noble Prophet, upon him be blessings and salutations, as mentioned in the ḥadīth:

كان جبريل يعرض عليه القرآن كل عام مرة فعرض عليه مرتين في العام الذي قبض

"Jibrīl would present the Qur'ān unto him once every year, and he presented it to him twice in the year he was taken away."
(Bukhārī: 4998)

INTRODUCTION

A memorization companion, be it in the form of a teacher, a friend, a parent, or even a spouse, can prove to be very beneficial in the process of Quranic memorization, and several of its benefits are immediately apparent. Primarily, the presence of a companion in this journey provides the benefit of motivation – man finds more of a drive to enact goodness when he finds a community with a common goal. Seeing the progress of others, drawing motivation from them, finding inspiration in their personal success, are all key motivating factors in one's own growth. Secondly, a companion provides the benefit of accountability – the learner does not remain alone in concern for his own results. His companion too remains in this concern and assists in diagnosing causes for not meeting memorization goals, if need be.

The purpose of the journal in your hands was designed with the intent of serving as an additional companion in this journey to further enhance the process of *ḥifẓ* by means of the following:

FEATURES

DAILY PROGRESS LOGS	
SCORE	Each daily entry features a field for a score. This score is for the assignment recited on the current day typically assigned the day prior.
NEW ASSIGNMENT	The daily entry also features fields labeled sūrah and ʿāyahs. This is for the assignment of the new lesson, to be recited in the next class.
TEACHER COMMENTS	The teacher comments section has been established for the convenience of the teacher. It may be used to explain the score given to the student for their recitation, express any concerns, highlight any errors, give any necessary information to guardians, or however the teacher may wish to use it.
REVIEW ASSIGNMENT	The review assignment field is to establish and record what the student has reviewed and what remains to review. To grade the quality of the review, a field has been provided next to the review assignment.
SIGNATURE	A field for a signature has also been provided. This signature should be the signature of the companion. The companion should oversee the student's progress and aid him in filling the gaps of his learning. The signature is a form of affirming that the companion has looked over the student's day-to-day progress.
PROGRESS TRACKER	The journal also includes a progress tracker which has been organized according to juzʾ, sūrah, and ʿāyah. This enables the student to visualize his progress. Every ʿāyah colored in gives a sense of growing a step closer to the destination of completion, further encouraging the student to continue and persevere despite any difficulty or struggle faced in this path.

This journal was designed to aid the teacher and student in the path of *ḥifẓ*, and the method of using the journal is solely on the style of the teacher. The methods aforementioned are but recommendations. I make *duʿāʾ* that this project proves to be beneficial in the *madāris* of the ʿAhl al-Sunnah, and that Allāh blesses all those who have worked towards this project, in any way, especially Muftī Sayyid ʿAsad al-Qādirī, whose modesty pushes him behind the curtain as he seeks to give me undeserved credit for this task.

His Sinning Slave,
Faqīr Sayyid ʿAbdul Ṣamad al-Qādirī (May he be pardoned)

PROGRESS LOGS

DATE :	SCORE :	
SURAH :	AYAHS :	S I G N A T U R E
TEACHER COMMENTS :		
REVIEW ASSIGNMENT :	GRADE :	

DATE :	SCORE :	
SURAH :	AYAHS :	S I G N A T U R E
TEACHER COMMENTS :		
REVIEW ASSIGNMENT :	GRADE :	

DATE :	SCORE :	
SURAH :	AYAHS :	S I G N A T U R E
TEACHER COMMENTS :		
REVIEW ASSIGNMENT :	GRADE :	

DATE :	SCORE :	
SURAH :	AYAHS :	S I G N A T U R E
TEACHER COMMENTS :		
REVIEW ASSIGNMENT :	GRADE :	

DATE :	SCORE :	
SURAH :	AYAHS :	S I G N A T U R E
TEACHER COMMENTS :		
REVIEW ASSIGNMENT :	GRADE :	

PROGRESS LOGS

DATE :	SCORE :	
SURAH :	AYAHS :	
TEACHER COMMENTS :		SIGNATURE
REVIEW ASSIGNMENT :	GRADE :	

DATE :	SCORE :	
SURAH :	AYAHS :	
TEACHER COMMENTS :		SIGNATURE
REVIEW ASSIGNMENT :	GRADE :	

DATE :	SCORE :	
SURAH :	AYAHS :	
TEACHER COMMENTS :		SIGNATURE
REVIEW ASSIGNMENT :	GRADE :	

DATE :	SCORE :	
SURAH :	AYAHS :	
TEACHER COMMENTS :		SIGNATURE
REVIEW ASSIGNMENT :	GRADE :	

DATE :	SCORE :	
SURAH :	AYAHS :	
TEACHER COMMENTS :		SIGNATURE
REVIEW ASSIGNMENT :	GRADE :	

PROGRESS LOGS

DATE :		SCORE :	
SURAH :		AYAHS :	
TEACHER COMMENTS :			
REVIEW ASSIGNMENT :		GRADE :	

SIGNATURE

DATE :		SCORE :	
SURAH :		AYAHS :	
TEACHER COMMENTS :			
REVIEW ASSIGNMENT :		GRADE :	

SIGNATURE

DATE :		SCORE :	
SURAH :		AYAHS :	
TEACHER COMMENTS :			
REVIEW ASSIGNMENT :		GRADE :	

SIGNATURE

DATE :		SCORE :	
SURAH :		AYAHS :	
TEACHER COMMENTS :			
REVIEW ASSIGNMENT :		GRADE :	

SIGNATURE

DATE :		SCORE :	
SURAH :		AYAHS :	
TEACHER COMMENTS :			
REVIEW ASSIGNMENT :		GRADE :	

SIGNATURE

PROGRESS LOGS

DATE :	SCORE :	
SURAH :	AYAHS :	
TEACHER COMMENTS :		SIGNATURE
REVIEW ASSIGNMENT :	GRADE :	

DATE :	SCORE :	
SURAH :	AYAHS :	
TEACHER COMMENTS :		SIGNATURE
REVIEW ASSIGNMENT :	GRADE :	

DATE :	SCORE :	
SURAH :	AYAHS :	
TEACHER COMMENTS :		SIGNATURE
REVIEW ASSIGNMENT :	GRADE :	

DATE :	SCORE :	
SURAH :	AYAHS :	
TEACHER COMMENTS :		SIGNATURE
REVIEW ASSIGNMENT :	GRADE :	

DATE :	SCORE :	
SURAH :	AYAHS :	
TEACHER COMMENTS :		SIGNATURE
REVIEW ASSIGNMENT :	GRADE :	

PROGRESS LOGS

DATE :	SCORE :	
SURAH :	AYAHS :	**SIGNATURE**
TEACHER COMMENTS :		
REVIEW ASSIGNMENT :	GRADE :	

DATE :	SCORE :	
SURAH :	AYAHS :	**SIGNATURE**
TEACHER COMMENTS :		
REVIEW ASSIGNMENT :	GRADE :	

DATE :	SCORE :	
SURAH :	AYAHS :	**SIGNATURE**
TEACHER COMMENTS :		
REVIEW ASSIGNMENT :	GRADE :	

DATE :	SCORE :	
SURAH :	AYAHS :	**SIGNATURE**
TEACHER COMMENTS :		
REVIEW ASSIGNMENT :	GRADE :	

DATE :	SCORE :	
SURAH :	AYAHS :	**SIGNATURE**
TEACHER COMMENTS :		
REVIEW ASSIGNMENT :	GRADE :	

PROGRESS LOGS

DATE :	SCORE :
SURAH :	AYAHS :
TEACHER COMMENTS :	
REVIEW ASSIGNMENT :	GRADE :

SIGNATURE

DATE :	SCORE :
SURAH :	AYAHS :
TEACHER COMMENTS :	
REVIEW ASSIGNMENT :	GRADE :

SIGNATURE

DATE :	SCORE :
SURAH :	AYAHS :
TEACHER COMMENTS :	
REVIEW ASSIGNMENT :	GRADE :

SIGNATURE

DATE :	SCORE :
SURAH :	AYAHS :
TEACHER COMMENTS :	
REVIEW ASSIGNMENT :	GRADE :

SIGNATURE

DATE :	SCORE :
SURAH :	AYAHS :
TEACHER COMMENTS :	
REVIEW ASSIGNMENT :	GRADE :

SIGNATURE

PROGRESS LOGS

DATE :		SCORE :	
SURAH :		AYAHS :	
TEACHER COMMENTS :			
REVIEW ASSIGNMENT :		GRADE :	

SIGNATURE

DATE :		SCORE :	
SURAH :		AYAHS :	
TEACHER COMMENTS :			
REVIEW ASSIGNMENT :		GRADE :	

SIGNATURE

DATE :		SCORE :	
SURAH :		AYAHS :	
TEACHER COMMENTS :			
REVIEW ASSIGNMENT :		GRADE :	

SIGNATURE

DATE :		SCORE :	
SURAH :		AYAHS :	
TEACHER COMMENTS :			
REVIEW ASSIGNMENT :		GRADE :	

SIGNATURE

DATE :		SCORE :	
SURAH :		AYAHS :	
TEACHER COMMENTS :			
REVIEW ASSIGNMENT :		GRADE :	

SIGNATURE

PROGRESS LOGS

DATE :	SCORE :
SURAH :	AYAHS :
TEACHER COMMENTS :	
REVIEW ASSIGNMENT :	GRADE :

SIGNATURE

DATE :	SCORE :
SURAH :	AYAHS :
TEACHER COMMENTS :	
REVIEW ASSIGNMENT :	GRADE :

SIGNATURE

DATE :	SCORE :
SURAH :	AYAHS :
TEACHER COMMENTS :	
REVIEW ASSIGNMENT :	GRADE :

SIGNATURE

DATE :	SCORE :
SURAH :	AYAHS :
TEACHER COMMENTS :	
REVIEW ASSIGNMENT :	GRADE :

SIGNATURE

DATE :	SCORE :
SURAH :	AYAHS :
TEACHER COMMENTS :	
REVIEW ASSIGNMENT :	GRADE :

SIGNATURE

PROGRESS LOGS

DATE :	SCORE :
SURAH :	AYAHS :
TEACHER COMMENTS :	
REVIEW ASSIGNMENT :	GRADE :

SIGNATURE

DATE :	SCORE :
SURAH :	AYAHS :
TEACHER COMMENTS :	
REVIEW ASSIGNMENT :	GRADE :

SIGNATURE

DATE :	SCORE :
SURAH :	AYAHS :
TEACHER COMMENTS :	
REVIEW ASSIGNMENT :	GRADE :

SIGNATURE

DATE :	SCORE :
SURAH :	AYAHS :
TEACHER COMMENTS :	
REVIEW ASSIGNMENT :	GRADE :

SIGNATURE

DATE :	SCORE :
SURAH :	AYAHS :
TEACHER COMMENTS :	
REVIEW ASSIGNMENT :	GRADE :

SIGNATURE

PROGRESS LOGS

DATE :	**SCORE :**
SURAH :	**AYAHS :**
TEACHER COMMENTS :	
REVIEW ASSIGNMENT :	**GRADE :**

SIGNATURE

DATE :	**SCORE :**
SURAH :	**AYAHS :**
TEACHER COMMENTS :	
REVIEW ASSIGNMENT :	**GRADE :**

SIGNATURE

DATE :	**SCORE :**
SURAH :	**AYAHS :**
TEACHER COMMENTS :	
REVIEW ASSIGNMENT :	**GRADE :**

SIGNATURE

DATE :	**SCORE :**
SURAH :	**AYAHS :**
TEACHER COMMENTS :	
REVIEW ASSIGNMENT :	**GRADE :**

SIGNATURE

DATE :	**SCORE :**
SURAH :	**AYAHS :**
TEACHER COMMENTS :	
REVIEW ASSIGNMENT :	**GRADE :**

SIGNATURE

PROGRESS LOGS

DATE :	SCORE :	
SURAH :	AYAHS :	SIGNATURE
TEACHER COMMENTS :		
REVIEW ASSIGNMENT :	GRADE :	

DATE :	SCORE :	
SURAH :	AYAHS :	SIGNATURE
TEACHER COMMENTS :		
REVIEW ASSIGNMENT :	GRADE :	

DATE :	SCORE :	
SURAH :	AYAHS :	SIGNATURE
TEACHER COMMENTS :		
REVIEW ASSIGNMENT :	GRADE :	

DATE :	SCORE :	
SURAH :	AYAHS :	SIGNATURE
TEACHER COMMENTS :		
REVIEW ASSIGNMENT :	GRADE :	

DATE :	SCORE :	
SURAH :	AYAHS :	SIGNATURE
TEACHER COMMENTS :		
REVIEW ASSIGNMENT :	GRADE :	

PROGRESS LOGS

DATE :	SCORE :	
SURAH :	AYAHS :	S
TEACHER COMMENTS :		I G N A T U R E
REVIEW ASSIGNMENT :	GRADE :	

DATE :	SCORE :	
SURAH :	AYAHS :	S I G N A T U R E
TEACHER COMMENTS :		
REVIEW ASSIGNMENT :	GRADE :	

DATE :	SCORE :	
SURAH :	AYAHS :	S I G N A T U R E
TEACHER COMMENTS :		
REVIEW ASSIGNMENT :	GRADE :	

DATE :	SCORE :	
SURAH :	AYAHS :	S I G N A T U R E
TEACHER COMMENTS :		
REVIEW ASSIGNMENT :	GRADE :	

DATE :	SCORE :	
SURAH :	AYAHS :	S I G N A T U R E
TEACHER COMMENTS :		
REVIEW ASSIGNMENT :	GRADE :	

PROGRESS LOGS

DATE :	SCORE :
SURAH :	AYAHS :
TEACHER COMMENTS :	
REVIEW ASSIGNMENT :	GRADE :

SIGNATURE

DATE :	SCORE :
SURAH :	AYAHS :
TEACHER COMMENTS :	
REVIEW ASSIGNMENT :	GRADE :

SIGNATURE

DATE :	SCORE :
SURAH :	AYAHS :
TEACHER COMMENTS :	
REVIEW ASSIGNMENT :	GRADE :

SIGNATURE

DATE :	SCORE :
SURAH :	AYAHS :
TEACHER COMMENTS :	
REVIEW ASSIGNMENT :	GRADE :

SIGNATURE

DATE :	SCORE :
SURAH :	AYAHS :
TEACHER COMMENTS :	
REVIEW ASSIGNMENT :	GRADE :

SIGNATURE

PROGRESS LOGS

DATE :	SCORE :
SURAH :	AYAHS :
TEACHER COMMENTS :	
REVIEW ASSIGNMENT :	GRADE :

SIGNATURE

DATE :	SCORE :
SURAH :	AYAHS :
TEACHER COMMENTS :	
REVIEW ASSIGNMENT :	GRADE :

SIGNATURE

DATE :	SCORE :
SURAH :	AYAHS :
TEACHER COMMENTS :	
REVIEW ASSIGNMENT :	GRADE :

SIGNATURE

DATE :	SCORE :
SURAH :	AYAHS :
TEACHER COMMENTS :	
REVIEW ASSIGNMENT :	GRADE :

SIGNATURE

DATE :	SCORE :
SURAH :	AYAHS :
TEACHER COMMENTS :	
REVIEW ASSIGNMENT :	GRADE :

SIGNATURE

PROGRESS LOGS

DATE :	SCORE :	
SURAH :	AYAHS :	
TEACHER COMMENTS :		SIGNATURE
REVIEW ASSIGNMENT :	GRADE :	

DATE :	SCORE :	
SURAH :	AYAHS :	
TEACHER COMMENTS :		SIGNATURE
REVIEW ASSIGNMENT :	GRADE :	

DATE :	SCORE :	
SURAH :	AYAHS :	
TEACHER COMMENTS :		SIGNATURE
REVIEW ASSIGNMENT :	GRADE :	

DATE :	SCORE :	
SURAH :	AYAHS :	
TEACHER COMMENTS :		SIGNATURE
REVIEW ASSIGNMENT :	GRADE :	

DATE :	SCORE :	
SURAH :	AYAHS :	
TEACHER COMMENTS :		SIGNATURE
REVIEW ASSIGNMENT :	GRADE :	

PROGRESS LOGS

DATE :	SCORE :
SURAH :	AYAHS :
TEACHER COMMENTS :	
REVIEW ASSIGNMENT :	GRADE :

SIGNATURE

DATE :	SCORE :
SURAH :	AYAHS :
TEACHER COMMENTS :	
REVIEW ASSIGNMENT :	GRADE :

SIGNATURE

DATE :	SCORE :
SURAH :	AYAHS :
TEACHER COMMENTS :	
REVIEW ASSIGNMENT :	GRADE :

SIGNATURE

DATE :	SCORE :
SURAH :	AYAHS :
TEACHER COMMENTS :	
REVIEW ASSIGNMENT :	GRADE :

SIGNATURE

DATE :	SCORE :
SURAH :	AYAHS :
TEACHER COMMENTS :	
REVIEW ASSIGNMENT :	GRADE :

SIGNATURE

PROGRESS LOGS

DATE :	SCORE :	
SURAH :	AYAHS :	
TEACHER COMMENTS :		SIGNATURE
REVIEW ASSIGNMENT :	GRADE :	

DATE :	SCORE :	
SURAH :	AYAHS :	
TEACHER COMMENTS :		SIGNATURE
REVIEW ASSIGNMENT :	GRADE :	

DATE :	SCORE :	
SURAH :	AYAHS :	
TEACHER COMMENTS :		SIGNATURE
REVIEW ASSIGNMENT :	GRADE :	

DATE :	SCORE :	
SURAH :	AYAHS :	
TEACHER COMMENTS :		SIGNATURE
REVIEW ASSIGNMENT :	GRADE :	

DATE :	SCORE :	
SURAH :	AYAHS :	
TEACHER COMMENTS :		SIGNATURE
REVIEW ASSIGNMENT :	GRADE :	

PROGRESS LOGS

DATE :	SCORE :
SURAH :	AYAHS :
TEACHER COMMENTS :	
REVIEW ASSIGNMENT :	GRADE :

SIGNATURE

DATE :	SCORE :
SURAH :	AYAHS :
TEACHER COMMENTS :	
REVIEW ASSIGNMENT :	GRADE :

SIGNATURE

DATE :	SCORE :
SURAH :	AYAHS :
TEACHER COMMENTS :	
REVIEW ASSIGNMENT :	GRADE :

SIGNATURE

DATE :	SCORE :
SURAH :	AYAHS :
TEACHER COMMENTS :	
REVIEW ASSIGNMENT :	GRADE :

SIGNATURE

DATE :	SCORE :
SURAH :	AYAHS :
TEACHER COMMENTS :	
REVIEW ASSIGNMENT :	GRADE :

SIGNATURE

PROGRESS LOGS

DATE :	SCORE :
SURAH :	AYAHS :
TEACHER COMMENTS :	
REVIEW ASSIGNMENT :	GRADE :

SIGNATURE

DATE :	SCORE :
SURAH :	AYAHS :
TEACHER COMMENTS :	
REVIEW ASSIGNMENT :	GRADE :

SIGNATURE

DATE :	SCORE :
SURAH :	AYAHS :
TEACHER COMMENTS :	
REVIEW ASSIGNMENT :	GRADE :

SIGNATURE

DATE :	SCORE :
SURAH :	AYAHS :
TEACHER COMMENTS :	
REVIEW ASSIGNMENT :	GRADE :

SIGNATURE

DATE :	SCORE :
SURAH :	AYAHS :
TEACHER COMMENTS :	
REVIEW ASSIGNMENT :	GRADE :

SIGNATURE

PROGRESS LOGS

DATE :	SCORE :	
SURAH :	AYAHS :	
TEACHER COMMENTS :		SIGNATURE
REVIEW ASSIGNMENT :	GRADE :	

DATE :	SCORE :	
SURAH :	AYAHS :	
TEACHER COMMENTS :		SIGNATURE
REVIEW ASSIGNMENT :	GRADE :	

DATE :	SCORE :	
SURAH :	AYAHS :	
TEACHER COMMENTS :		SIGNATURE
REVIEW ASSIGNMENT :	GRADE :	

DATE :	SCORE :	
SURAH :	AYAHS :	
TEACHER COMMENTS :		SIGNATURE
REVIEW ASSIGNMENT :	GRADE :	

DATE :	SCORE :	
SURAH :	AYAHS :	
TEACHER COMMENTS :		SIGNATURE
REVIEW ASSIGNMENT :	GRADE :	

PROGRESS LOGS

DATE :	SCORE :
SURAH :	AYAHS :
TEACHER COMMENTS :	
REVIEW ASSIGNMENT :	GRADE :

SIGNATURE

DATE :	SCORE :
SURAH :	AYAHS :
TEACHER COMMENTS :	
REVIEW ASSIGNMENT :	GRADE :

SIGNATURE

DATE :	SCORE :
SURAH :	AYAHS :
TEACHER COMMENTS :	
REVIEW ASSIGNMENT :	GRADE :

SIGNATURE

DATE :	SCORE :
SURAH :	AYAHS :
TEACHER COMMENTS :	
REVIEW ASSIGNMENT :	GRADE :

SIGNATURE

DATE :	SCORE :
SURAH :	AYAHS :
TEACHER COMMENTS :	
REVIEW ASSIGNMENT :	GRADE :

SIGNATURE

PROGRESS LOGS

DATE :	SCORE :	
SURAH :	AYAHS :	
TEACHER COMMENTS :		SIGNATURE
REVIEW ASSIGNMENT :	GRADE :	

DATE :	SCORE :	
SURAH :	AYAHS :	
TEACHER COMMENTS :		SIGNATURE
REVIEW ASSIGNMENT :	GRADE :	

DATE :	SCORE :	
SURAH :	AYAHS :	
TEACHER COMMENTS :		SIGNATURE
REVIEW ASSIGNMENT :	GRADE :	

DATE :	SCORE :	
SURAH :	AYAHS :	
TEACHER COMMENTS :		SIGNATURE
REVIEW ASSIGNMENT :	GRADE :	

DATE :	SCORE :	
SURAH :	AYAHS :	
TEACHER COMMENTS :		SIGNATURE
REVIEW ASSIGNMENT :	GRADE :	

PROGRESS LOGS

DATE :	SCORE :
SURAH :	AYAHS :
TEACHER COMMENTS :	
REVIEW ASSIGNMENT :	GRADE :

SIGNATURE

DATE :	SCORE :
SURAH :	AYAHS :
TEACHER COMMENTS :	
REVIEW ASSIGNMENT :	GRADE :

SIGNATURE

DATE :	SCORE :
SURAH :	AYAHS :
TEACHER COMMENTS :	
REVIEW ASSIGNMENT :	GRADE :

SIGNATURE

DATE :	SCORE :
SURAH :	AYAHS :
TEACHER COMMENTS :	
REVIEW ASSIGNMENT :	GRADE :

SIGNATURE

DATE :	SCORE :
SURAH :	AYAHS :
TEACHER COMMENTS :	
REVIEW ASSIGNMENT :	GRADE :

SIGNATURE

PROGRESS LOGS

DATE :	SCORE :
SURAH :	AYAHS :
TEACHER COMMENTS :	
REVIEW ASSIGNMENT :	GRADE :

SIGNATURE

DATE :	SCORE :
SURAH :	AYAHS :
TEACHER COMMENTS :	
REVIEW ASSIGNMENT :	GRADE :

SIGNATURE

DATE :	SCORE :
SURAH :	AYAHS :
TEACHER COMMENTS :	
REVIEW ASSIGNMENT :	GRADE :

SIGNATURE

DATE :	SCORE :
SURAH :	AYAHS :
TEACHER COMMENTS :	
REVIEW ASSIGNMENT :	GRADE :

SIGNATURE

DATE :	SCORE :
SURAH :	AYAHS :
TEACHER COMMENTS :	
REVIEW ASSIGNMENT :	GRADE :

SIGNATURE

PROGRESS LOGS

DATE :	SCORE :	
SURAH :	AYAHS :	SIGNATURE
TEACHER COMMENTS :		
REVIEW ASSIGNMENT :	GRADE :	

DATE :	SCORE :	
SURAH :	AYAHS :	SIGNATURE
TEACHER COMMENTS :		
REVIEW ASSIGNMENT :	GRADE :	

DATE :	SCORE :	
SURAH :	AYAHS :	SIGNATURE
TEACHER COMMENTS :		
REVIEW ASSIGNMENT :	GRADE :	

DATE :	SCORE :	
SURAH :	AYAHS :	SIGNATURE
TEACHER COMMENTS :		
REVIEW ASSIGNMENT :	GRADE :	

DATE :	SCORE :	
SURAH :	AYAHS :	SIGNATURE
TEACHER COMMENTS :		
REVIEW ASSIGNMENT :	GRADE :	

PROGRESS LOGS

DATE :	SCORE :	
SURAH :	AYAHS :	S
TEACHER COMMENTS :		I
		G
		N
REVIEW ASSIGNMENT :	GRADE :	A

DATE :	SCORE :
SURAH :	AYAHS :
TEACHER COMMENTS :	
REVIEW ASSIGNMENT :	GRADE :

DATE :	SCORE :
SURAH :	AYAHS :
TEACHER COMMENTS :	
REVIEW ASSIGNMENT :	GRADE :

DATE :	SCORE :
SURAH :	AYAHS :
TEACHER COMMENTS :	
REVIEW ASSIGNMENT :	GRADE :

DATE :	SCORE :
SURAH :	AYAHS :
TEACHER COMMENTS :	
REVIEW ASSIGNMENT :	GRADE :

SIGNATURE

PROGRESS LOGS

DATE :	SCORE :	
SURAH :	AYAHS :	SIGNATURE
TEACHER COMMENTS :		
REVIEW ASSIGNMENT :	GRADE :	

DATE :	SCORE :	
SURAH :	AYAHS :	SIGNATURE
TEACHER COMMENTS :		
REVIEW ASSIGNMENT :	GRADE :	

DATE :	SCORE :	
SURAH :	AYAHS :	SIGNATURE
TEACHER COMMENTS :		
REVIEW ASSIGNMENT :	GRADE :	

DATE :	SCORE :	
SURAH :	AYAHS :	SIGNATURE
TEACHER COMMENTS :		
REVIEW ASSIGNMENT :	GRADE :	

DATE :	SCORE :	
SURAH :	AYAHS :	SIGNATURE
TEACHER COMMENTS :		
REVIEW ASSIGNMENT :	GRADE :	

PROGRESS LOGS

DATE :	SCORE :	
SURAH :	AYAHS :	SIGNATURE
TEACHER COMMENTS :		
REVIEW ASSIGNMENT :	GRADE :	

DATE :	SCORE :	
SURAH :	AYAHS :	SIGNATURE
TEACHER COMMENTS :		
REVIEW ASSIGNMENT :	GRADE :	

DATE :	SCORE :	
SURAH :	AYAHS :	SIGNATURE
TEACHER COMMENTS :		
REVIEW ASSIGNMENT :	GRADE :	

DATE :	SCORE :	
SURAH :	AYAHS :	SIGNATURE
TEACHER COMMENTS :		
REVIEW ASSIGNMENT :	GRADE :	

DATE :	SCORE :	
SURAH :	AYAHS :	SIGNATURE
TEACHER COMMENTS :		
REVIEW ASSIGNMENT :	GRADE :	

PROGRESS LOGS

DATE :	SCORE :
SURAH :	AYAHS :
TEACHER COMMENTS :	
REVIEW ASSIGNMENT :	GRADE :

SIGNATURE

DATE :	SCORE :
SURAH :	AYAHS :
TEACHER COMMENTS :	
REVIEW ASSIGNMENT :	GRADE :

SIGNATURE

DATE :	SCORE :
SURAH :	AYAHS :
TEACHER COMMENTS :	
REVIEW ASSIGNMENT :	GRADE :

SIGNATURE

DATE :	SCORE :
SURAH :	AYAHS :
TEACHER COMMENTS :	
REVIEW ASSIGNMENT :	GRADE :

SIGNATURE

DATE :	SCORE :
SURAH :	AYAHS :
TEACHER COMMENTS :	
REVIEW ASSIGNMENT :	GRADE :

SIGNATURE

PROGRESS LOGS

DATE :	SCORE :	
SURAH :	AYAHS :	
TEACHER COMMENTS :		SIGNATURE
REVIEW ASSIGNMENT :	GRADE :	

DATE :	SCORE :	
SURAH :	AYAHS :	
TEACHER COMMENTS :		SIGNATURE
REVIEW ASSIGNMENT :	GRADE :	

DATE :	SCORE :	
SURAH :	AYAHS :	
TEACHER COMMENTS :		SIGNATURE
REVIEW ASSIGNMENT :	GRADE :	

DATE :	SCORE :	
SURAH :	AYAHS :	
TEACHER COMMENTS :		SIGNATURE
REVIEW ASSIGNMENT :	GRADE :	

DATE :	SCORE :	
SURAH :	AYAHS :	
TEACHER COMMENTS :		SIGNATURE
REVIEW ASSIGNMENT :	GRADE :	

PROGRESS LOGS

DATE :	SCORE :	
SURAH :	AYAHS :	
TEACHER COMMENTS :		SIGNATURE
REVIEW ASSIGNMENT :	GRADE :	

DATE :	SCORE :	
SURAH :	AYAHS :	
TEACHER COMMENTS :		SIGNATURE
REVIEW ASSIGNMENT :	GRADE :	

DATE :	SCORE :	
SURAH :	AYAHS :	
TEACHER COMMENTS :		SIGNATURE
REVIEW ASSIGNMENT :	GRADE :	

DATE :	SCORE :	
SURAH :	AYAHS :	
TEACHER COMMENTS :		SIGNATURE
REVIEW ASSIGNMENT :	GRADE :	

DATE :	SCORE :	
SURAH :	AYAHS :	
TEACHER COMMENTS :		SIGNATURE
REVIEW ASSIGNMENT :	GRADE :	

PROGRESS LOGS

DATE :	SCORE :	
SURAH :	AYAHS :	
TEACHER COMMENTS :		SIGNATURE
REVIEW ASSIGNMENT :	GRADE :	

DATE :	SCORE :	
SURAH :	AYAHS :	
TEACHER COMMENTS :		SIGNATURE
REVIEW ASSIGNMENT :	GRADE :	

DATE :	SCORE :	
SURAH :	AYAHS :	
TEACHER COMMENTS :		SIGNATURE
REVIEW ASSIGNMENT :	GRADE :	

DATE :	SCORE :	
SURAH :	AYAHS :	
TEACHER COMMENTS :		SIGNATURE
REVIEW ASSIGNMENT :	GRADE :	

DATE :	SCORE :	
SURAH :	AYAHS :	
TEACHER COMMENTS :		SIGNATURE
REVIEW ASSIGNMENT :	GRADE :	

PROGRESS LOGS

DATE :	SCORE :
SURAH :	AYAHS :
TEACHER COMMENTS :	
REVIEW ASSIGNMENT :	GRADE :

SIGNATURE

DATE :	SCORE :
SURAH :	AYAHS :
TEACHER COMMENTS :	
REVIEW ASSIGNMENT :	GRADE :

SIGNATURE

DATE :	SCORE :
SURAH :	AYAHS :
TEACHER COMMENTS :	
REVIEW ASSIGNMENT :	GRADE :

SIGNATURE

DATE :	SCORE :
SURAH :	AYAHS :
TEACHER COMMENTS :	
REVIEW ASSIGNMENT :	GRADE :

SIGNATURE

DATE :	SCORE :
SURAH :	AYAHS :
TEACHER COMMENTS :	
REVIEW ASSIGNMENT :	GRADE :

SIGNATURE

PROGRESS LOGS

DATE :	SCORE :
SURAH :	AYAHS :
TEACHER COMMENTS :	
REVIEW ASSIGNMENT :	GRADE :

SIGNATURE

DATE :	SCORE :
SURAH :	AYAHS :
TEACHER COMMENTS :	
REVIEW ASSIGNMENT :	GRADE :

SIGNATURE

DATE :	SCORE :
SURAH :	AYAHS :
TEACHER COMMENTS :	
REVIEW ASSIGNMENT :	GRADE :

SIGNATURE

DATE :	SCORE :
SURAH :	AYAHS :
TEACHER COMMENTS :	
REVIEW ASSIGNMENT :	GRADE :

SIGNATURE

DATE :	SCORE :
SURAH :	AYAHS :
TEACHER COMMENTS :	
REVIEW ASSIGNMENT :	GRADE :

SIGNATURE

PROGRESS LOGS

DATE :	SCORE :
SURAH :	AYAHS :
TEACHER COMMENTS :	
REVIEW ASSIGNMENT :	GRADE :

SIGNATURE

DATE :	SCORE :
SURAH :	AYAHS :
TEACHER COMMENTS :	
REVIEW ASSIGNMENT :	GRADE :

SIGNATURE

DATE :	SCORE :
SURAH :	AYAHS :
TEACHER COMMENTS :	
REVIEW ASSIGNMENT :	GRADE :

SIGNATURE

DATE :	SCORE :
SURAH :	AYAHS :
TEACHER COMMENTS :	
REVIEW ASSIGNMENT :	GRADE :

SIGNATURE

DATE :	SCORE :
SURAH :	AYAHS :
TEACHER COMMENTS :	
REVIEW ASSIGNMENT :	GRADE :

SIGNATURE

PROGRESS LOGS

DATE :	SCORE :	
SURAH :	AYAHS :	
TEACHER COMMENTS :		SIGNATURE
REVIEW ASSIGNMENT :	GRADE :	

DATE :	SCORE :	
SURAH :	AYAHS :	
TEACHER COMMENTS :		SIGNATURE
REVIEW ASSIGNMENT :	GRADE :	

DATE :	SCORE :	
SURAH :	AYAHS :	
TEACHER COMMENTS :		SIGNATURE
REVIEW ASSIGNMENT :	GRADE :	

DATE :	SCORE :	
SURAH :	AYAHS :	
TEACHER COMMENTS :		SIGNATURE
REVIEW ASSIGNMENT :	GRADE :	

DATE :	SCORE :	
SURAH :	AYAHS :	
TEACHER COMMENTS :		SIGNATURE
REVIEW ASSIGNMENT :	GRADE :	

PROGRESS LOGS

DATE :	SCORE :
SURAH :	AYAHS :
TEACHER COMMENTS :	
REVIEW ASSIGNMENT :	GRADE :

SIGNATURE

DATE :	SCORE :
SURAH :	AYAHS :
TEACHER COMMENTS :	
REVIEW ASSIGNMENT :	GRADE :

SIGNATURE

DATE :	SCORE :
SURAH :	AYAHS :
TEACHER COMMENTS :	
REVIEW ASSIGNMENT :	GRADE :

SIGNATURE

DATE :	SCORE :
SURAH :	AYAHS :
TEACHER COMMENTS :	
REVIEW ASSIGNMENT :	GRADE :

SIGNATURE

DATE :	SCORE :
SURAH :	AYAHS :
TEACHER COMMENTS :	
REVIEW ASSIGNMENT :	GRADE :

SIGNATURE

PROGRESS LOGS

DATE :	SCORE :	
SURAH :	AYAHS :	
TEACHER COMMENTS :		SIGNATURE
REVIEW ASSIGNMENT :	GRADE :	

DATE :	SCORE :	
SURAH :	AYAHS :	
TEACHER COMMENTS :		SIGNATURE
REVIEW ASSIGNMENT :	GRADE :	

DATE :	SCORE :	
SURAH :	AYAHS :	
TEACHER COMMENTS :		SIGNATURE
REVIEW ASSIGNMENT :	GRADE :	

DATE :	SCORE :	
SURAH :	AYAHS :	
TEACHER COMMENTS :		SIGNATURE
REVIEW ASSIGNMENT :	GRADE :	

DATE :	SCORE :	
SURAH :	AYAHS :	
TEACHER COMMENTS :		SIGNATURE
REVIEW ASSIGNMENT :	GRADE :	

PROGRESS LOGS

DATE :	SCORE :
SURAH :	AYAHS :
TEACHER COMMENTS :	
REVIEW ASSIGNMENT :	GRADE :

SIGNATURE

DATE :	SCORE :
SURAH :	AYAHS :
TEACHER COMMENTS :	
REVIEW ASSIGNMENT :	GRADE :

SIGNATURE

DATE :	SCORE :
SURAH :	AYAHS :
TEACHER COMMENTS :	
REVIEW ASSIGNMENT :	GRADE :

SIGNATURE

DATE :	SCORE :
SURAH :	AYAHS :
TEACHER COMMENTS :	
REVIEW ASSIGNMENT :	GRADE :

SIGNATURE

DATE :	SCORE :
SURAH :	AYAHS :
TEACHER COMMENTS :	
REVIEW ASSIGNMENT :	GRADE :

SIGNATURE

PROGRESS LOGS

DATE :	SCORE :	
SURAH :	AYAHS :	S I G N A T U R E
TEACHER COMMENTS :		
REVIEW ASSIGNMENT :	GRADE :	

DATE :	SCORE :	
SURAH :	AYAHS :	S I G N A T U R E
TEACHER COMMENTS :		
REVIEW ASSIGNMENT :	GRADE :	

DATE :	SCORE :	
SURAH :	AYAHS :	S I G N A T U R E
TEACHER COMMENTS :		
REVIEW ASSIGNMENT :	GRADE :	

DATE :	SCORE :	
SURAH :	AYAHS :	S I G N A T U R E
TEACHER COMMENTS :		
REVIEW ASSIGNMENT :	GRADE :	

DATE :	SCORE :	
SURAH :	AYAHS :	S I G N A T U R E
TEACHER COMMENTS :		
REVIEW ASSIGNMENT :	GRADE :	

PROGRESS LOGS

DATE :	SCORE :	
SURAH :	AYAHS :	
TEACHER COMMENTS :		SIGNATURE
REVIEW ASSIGNMENT :	GRADE :	

DATE :	SCORE :	
SURAH :	AYAHS :	
TEACHER COMMENTS :		SIGNATURE
REVIEW ASSIGNMENT :	GRADE :	

DATE :	SCORE :	
SURAH :	AYAHS :	
TEACHER COMMENTS :		SIGNATURE
REVIEW ASSIGNMENT :	GRADE :	

DATE :	SCORE :	
SURAH :	AYAHS :	
TEACHER COMMENTS :		SIGNATURE
REVIEW ASSIGNMENT :	GRADE :	

DATE :	SCORE :	
SURAH :	AYAHS :	
TEACHER COMMENTS :		SIGNATURE
REVIEW ASSIGNMENT :	GRADE :	

PROGRESS LOGS

DATE :	SCORE :
SURAH :	AYAHS :
TEACHER COMMENTS :	
REVIEW ASSIGNMENT :	GRADE :

SIGNATURE

DATE :	SCORE :
SURAH :	AYAHS :
TEACHER COMMENTS :	
REVIEW ASSIGNMENT :	GRADE :

SIGNATURE

DATE :	SCORE :
SURAH :	AYAHS :
TEACHER COMMENTS :	
REVIEW ASSIGNMENT :	GRADE :

SIGNATURE

DATE :	SCORE :
SURAH :	AYAHS :
TEACHER COMMENTS :	
REVIEW ASSIGNMENT :	GRADE :

SIGNATURE

DATE :	SCORE :
SURAH :	AYAHS :
TEACHER COMMENTS :	
REVIEW ASSIGNMENT :	GRADE :

SIGNATURE

PROGRESS LOGS

DATE :	SCORE :
SURAH :	AYAHS :
TEACHER COMMENTS :	
REVIEW ASSIGNMENT :	GRADE :

SIGNATURE

DATE :	SCORE :
SURAH :	AYAHS :
TEACHER COMMENTS :	
REVIEW ASSIGNMENT :	GRADE :

SIGNATURE

DATE :	SCORE :
SURAH :	AYAHS :
TEACHER COMMENTS :	
REVIEW ASSIGNMENT :	GRADE :

SIGNATURE

DATE :	SCORE :
SURAH :	AYAHS :
TEACHER COMMENTS :	
REVIEW ASSIGNMENT :	GRADE :

SIGNATURE

DATE :	SCORE :
SURAH :	AYAHS :
TEACHER COMMENTS :	
REVIEW ASSIGNMENT :	GRADE :

SIGNATURE

PROGRESS LOGS

DATE :	SCORE :	
SURAH :	AYAHS :	S
TEACHER COMMENTS :		I G N
		A T U R E
REVIEW ASSIGNMENT :	GRADE :	

DATE :	SCORE :	
SURAH :	AYAHS :	S
TEACHER COMMENTS :		I G N
		A T U R E
REVIEW ASSIGNMENT :	GRADE :	

DATE :	SCORE :	
SURAH :	AYAHS :	S
TEACHER COMMENTS :		I G N
		A T U R E
REVIEW ASSIGNMENT :	GRADE :	

DATE :	SCORE :	
SURAH :	AYAHS :	S
TEACHER COMMENTS :		I G N
		A T U R E
REVIEW ASSIGNMENT :	GRADE :	

DATE :	SCORE :	
SURAH :	AYAHS :	S
TEACHER COMMENTS :		I G N
		A T U R E
REVIEW ASSIGNMENT :	GRADE :	

PROGRESS LOGS

DATE :	SCORE :	
SURAH :	AYAHS :	S I G N A T U R E
TEACHER COMMENTS :		
REVIEW ASSIGNMENT :	GRADE :	

DATE :	SCORE :	
SURAH :	AYAHS :	S I G N A T U R E
TEACHER COMMENTS :		
REVIEW ASSIGNMENT :	GRADE :	

DATE :	SCORE :	
SURAH :	AYAHS :	S I G N A T U R E
TEACHER COMMENTS :		
REVIEW ASSIGNMENT :	GRADE :	

DATE :	SCORE :	
SURAH :	AYAHS :	S I G N A T U R E
TEACHER COMMENTS :		
REVIEW ASSIGNMENT :	GRADE :	

DATE :	SCORE :	
SURAH :	AYAHS :	S I G N A T U R E
TEACHER COMMENTS :		
REVIEW ASSIGNMENT :	GRADE :	

PROGRESS LOGS

DATE :	SCORE :	
SURAH :	AYAHS :	SIGNATURE
TEACHER COMMENTS :		
REVIEW ASSIGNMENT :	GRADE :	

DATE :	SCORE :	
SURAH :	AYAHS :	SIGNATURE
TEACHER COMMENTS :		
REVIEW ASSIGNMENT :	GRADE :	

DATE :	SCORE :	
SURAH :	AYAHS :	SIGNATURE
TEACHER COMMENTS :		
REVIEW ASSIGNMENT :	GRADE :	

DATE :	SCORE :	
SURAH :	AYAHS :	SIGNATURE
TEACHER COMMENTS :		
REVIEW ASSIGNMENT :	GRADE :	

DATE :	SCORE :	
SURAH :	AYAHS :	SIGNATURE
TEACHER COMMENTS :		
REVIEW ASSIGNMENT :	GRADE :	

PROGRESS LOGS

DATE :	SCORE :
SURAH :	AYAHS :
TEACHER COMMENTS :	
REVIEW ASSIGNMENT :	GRADE :

SIGNATURE

DATE :	SCORE :
SURAH :	AYAHS :
TEACHER COMMENTS :	
REVIEW ASSIGNMENT :	GRADE :

SIGNATURE

DATE :	SCORE :
SURAH :	AYAHS :
TEACHER COMMENTS :	
REVIEW ASSIGNMENT :	GRADE :

SIGNATURE

DATE :	SCORE :
SURAH :	AYAHS :
TEACHER COMMENTS :	
REVIEW ASSIGNMENT :	GRADE :

SIGNATURE

DATE :	SCORE :
SURAH :	AYAHS :
TEACHER COMMENTS :	
REVIEW ASSIGNMENT :	GRADE :

SIGNATURE

PROGRESS LOGS

DATE :	SCORE :	
SURAH :	AYAHS :	S I G N A T U R E
TEACHER COMMENTS :		
REVIEW ASSIGNMENT :	GRADE :	

DATE :	SCORE :	
SURAH :	AYAHS :	S I G N A T U R E
TEACHER COMMENTS :		
REVIEW ASSIGNMENT :	GRADE :	

DATE :	SCORE :	
SURAH :	AYAHS :	S I G N A T U R E
TEACHER COMMENTS :		
REVIEW ASSIGNMENT :	GRADE :	

DATE :	SCORE :	
SURAH :	AYAHS :	S I G N A T U R E
TEACHER COMMENTS :		
REVIEW ASSIGNMENT :	GRADE :	

DATE :	SCORE :	
SURAH :	AYAHS :	S I G N A T U R E
TEACHER COMMENTS :		
REVIEW ASSIGNMENT :	GRADE :	

PROGRESS LOGS

DATE :	SCORE :	
SURAH :	AYAHS :	
TEACHER COMMENTS :		**SIGNATURE**
REVIEW ASSIGNMENT :	GRADE :	

DATE :	SCORE :	
SURAH :	AYAHS :	
TEACHER COMMENTS :		**SIGNATURE**
REVIEW ASSIGNMENT :	GRADE :	

DATE :	SCORE :	
SURAH :	AYAHS :	
TEACHER COMMENTS :		**SIGNATURE**
REVIEW ASSIGNMENT :	GRADE :	

DATE :	SCORE :	
SURAH :	AYAHS :	
TEACHER COMMENTS :		**SIGNATURE**
REVIEW ASSIGNMENT :	GRADE :	

DATE :	SCORE :	
SURAH :	AYAHS :	
TEACHER COMMENTS :		**SIGNATURE**
REVIEW ASSIGNMENT :	GRADE :	

PROGRESS LOGS

DATE :	SCORE :
SURAH :	AYAHS :
TEACHER COMMENTS :	
REVIEW ASSIGNMENT :	GRADE :

SIGNATURE

DATE :	SCORE :
SURAH :	AYAHS :
TEACHER COMMENTS :	
REVIEW ASSIGNMENT :	GRADE :

SIGNATURE

DATE :	SCORE :
SURAH :	AYAHS :
TEACHER COMMENTS :	
REVIEW ASSIGNMENT :	GRADE :

SIGNATURE

DATE :	SCORE :
SURAH :	AYAHS :
TEACHER COMMENTS :	
REVIEW ASSIGNMENT :	GRADE :

SIGNATURE

DATE :	SCORE :
SURAH :	AYAHS :
TEACHER COMMENTS :	
REVIEW ASSIGNMENT :	GRADE :

SIGNATURE

PROGRESS LOGS

DATE :	SCORE :
SURAH :	AYAHS :
TEACHER COMMENTS :	
REVIEW ASSIGNMENT :	GRADE :

SIGNATURE

DATE :	SCORE :
SURAH :	AYAHS :
TEACHER COMMENTS :	
REVIEW ASSIGNMENT :	GRADE :

SIGNATURE

DATE :	SCORE :
SURAH :	AYAHS :
TEACHER COMMENTS :	
REVIEW ASSIGNMENT :	GRADE :

SIGNATURE

DATE :	SCORE :
SURAH :	AYAHS :
TEACHER COMMENTS :	
REVIEW ASSIGNMENT :	GRADE :

SIGNATURE

DATE :	SCORE :
SURAH :	AYAHS :
TEACHER COMMENTS :	
REVIEW ASSIGNMENT :	GRADE :

SIGNATURE

PROGRESS LOGS

DATE :	SCORE :
SURAH :	AYAHS :
TEACHER COMMENTS :	
REVIEW ASSIGNMENT :	GRADE :

SIGNATURE

DATE :	SCORE :
SURAH :	AYAHS :
TEACHER COMMENTS :	
REVIEW ASSIGNMENT :	GRADE :

SIGNATURE

DATE :	SCORE :
SURAH :	AYAHS :
TEACHER COMMENTS :	
REVIEW ASSIGNMENT :	GRADE :

SIGNATURE

DATE :	SCORE :
SURAH :	AYAHS :
TEACHER COMMENTS :	
REVIEW ASSIGNMENT :	GRADE :

SIGNATURE

DATE :	SCORE :
SURAH :	AYAHS :
TEACHER COMMENTS :	
REVIEW ASSIGNMENT :	GRADE :

SIGNATURE

PROGRESS TRACKER

SURAH AL-FATIHAH

JUZ #1 · SURAH #1

1	2	3	4	5	6	7

SURAH AL-BAQARAH

JUZ #1 · SURAH #2

1	2	3	4	5	6	7
8	9	10	11	12	13	14
15	16	17	18	19	20	21
22	23	24	25	26	27	28
29	30	31	32	33	34	35
36	37	38	39	40	41	42
43	44	45	46	47	48	49
50	51	52	53	54	55	56
57	58	59	60	61	62	63
64	65	66	67	68	69	70
71	72	73	74	75	76	77
78	79	80	81	82	83	84
85	86	87	88	89	90	91
92	93	94	95	96	97	98

SURAH AL-BAQARAH

99	100	101	102	103	104	105
106	107	108	109	110	111	112
113	114	115	116	117	118	119
120	121	122	123	124	125	126
127	128	129	130	131	132	133
134	135	136	137	138	139	140
141						

SURAH AL-BAQARAH

JUZ #2 · SURAH #2

142	143	144	145	146	147	148
149	150	151	152	153	154	155
156	157	158	159	160	161	162
163	164	165	166	167	168	169
170	171	172	173	174	175	176
177	178	179	180	181	182	183
184	185	186	187	188	189	190
191	192	193	194	195	196	197
198	199	200	201	202	203	204
205	206	207	208	209	210	211
212	213	214	215	216	217	218
219	220	221	222	223	224	225
226	227	228	229	230	231	232
233	234	235	236	237	238	239
240	241	242	243	244	245	246
247	248	249	250	251	252	

SURAH AL-BAQARAH

JUZ #3 • SURAH #2

253	254	255	256	257	258	259
260	261	262	263	264	265	266
267	268	269	270	271	272	273
274	275	276	277	278	279	280
281	282	283	284	285	286	

SURAH AL `IMRAN

JUZ #3 • SURAH #3

1	2	3	4	5	6	7
8	9	10	11	12	13	14
15	16	17	18	19	20	21
22	23	24	25	26	27	28
29	30	31	32	33	34	35
36	37	38	39	40	41	42
43	44	45	46	47	48	49
50	51	52	53	54	55	56
57	58	59	60	61	62	63
64	65	66	67	68	69	70

SURAH AL `IMRAN

71	72	73	74	75	76	77
78	79	80	81	82	83	84
85	86	87	88	89	90	91
92						

SURAH AL `IMRAN

JUZ #4 · SURAH #3

93	94	95	96	97	98	99
100	101	102	103	104	105	106
107	108	109	110	111	112	113
114	115	116	117	118	119	120
121	122	123	124	125	126	127
128	129	130	131	132	133	134
135	136	137	138	139	140	141
142	143	144	145	146	147	148
149	150	151	152	153	154	155
156	157	158	159	160	161	162
163	164	165	166	167	168	169
170	171	172	173	174	175	176
177	178	179	180	181	182	183
184	185	186	187	188	189	190
191	192	193	194	195	196	197
198	199	200				

SURAH AL-NISA

1	2	3	4	5	6	7
8	9	10	11	12	13	14
15	16	17	18	19	20	21
22	23					

SURAH AL-NISA

24	25	26	27	28	29	30
31	32	33	34	35	36	37
38	39	40	41	42	43	44
45	46	47	48	49	50	51
52	53	54	55	56	57	58
59	60	61	62	63	64	65
66	67	68	69	70	71	72
73	74	75	76	77	78	79
80	81	82	83	84	85	86
87	88	89	90	91	92	93
94	95	96	97	98	99	100
101	102	103	104	105	106	107
108	109	110	111	112	113	114
115	116	117	118	119	120	121
122	123	124	125	126	127	128
129	130	131	132	133	134	135

SURAH AL-NISA

136	137	138	139	140	141	142
143	144	145	146	147		

SURAH AL-NISA

JUZ #6 · SURAH #4

148	149	150	151	152	153	154
155	156	157	158	159	160	161
162	163	164	165	166	167	168
169	170	171	172	173	174	175
176						

SURAH AL-MA'IDAH

JUZ #6 · SURAH #5

1	2	3	4	5	6	7
8	9	10	11	12	13	14
15	16	17	18	19	20	21
22	23	24	25	26	27	28
29	30	31	32	33	34	35
36	37	38	39	40	41	42
43	44	45	46	47	48	49
50	51	52	53	54	55	56
57	58	59	60	61	62	63
64	65	66	67	68	69	70

SURAH AL-MA'IDAH

JUZ #6 · SURAH #5

71	72	73	74	75	76	77
78	79	80	81			

SURAH AL-MA'IDAH

JUZ #7 · SURAH #5

82	83	84	85	86	87	88
89	90	91	92	93	94	95
96	97	98	99	100	101	102
103	104	105	106	107	108	109
110	111	112	113	114	115	116
117	118	119	120			

SURAH AL-AN`AM

JUZ #7 · SURAH #6

1	2	3	4	5	6	7
8	9	10	11	12	13	14
15	16	17	18	19	20	21
22	23	24	25	26	27	28
29	30	31	32	33	34	35
36	37	38	39	40	41	42
43	44	45	46	47	48	49
50	51	52	53	54	55	56
57	58	59	60	61	62	63

SURAH AL-AN`AM

64	65	66	67	68	69	70
71	72	73	74	75	76	77
78	79	80	81	82	83	84
85	86	87	88	89	90	91
92	93	94	95	96	97	98
99	100	101	102	103	104	105
106	107	108	109	110		

SURAH AL-AN`AM

						JUZ #8 · SURAH #6
111	112	113	114	115	116	117
118	119	120	121	122	123	124
125	126	127	128	129	130	131
132	133	134	135	136	137	138
139	140	141	142	143	144	145
146	147	148	149	150	151	152
153	154	155	156	157	158	159
160	161	162	163	164	165	

SURAH AL-A`RAF

						JUZ #8 · SURAH #7
1	2	3	4	5	6	7
8	9	10	11	12	13	14
15	16	17	18	19	20	21
22	23	24	25	26	27	28
29	30	31	32	33	34	35
36	37	38	39	40	41	42
43	44	45	46	47	48	49

SURAH AL-A`RAF

50	51	52	53	54	55	56
57	58	59	60	61	62	63
64	65	66	67	68	69	70
71	72	73	74	75	76	77
78	79	80	81	82	83	84
85	86	87				

SURAH AL-A`RAF

88	89	90	91	92	93	94
95	96	97	98	99	100	101
102	103	104	105	106	107	108
109	110	111	112	113	114	115
116	117	118	119	120	121	122
123	124	125	126	127	128	129
130	131	132	133	134	135	136
137	138	139	140	141	142	143
144	145	146	147	148	149	150
151	152	153	154	155	156	157
158	159	160	161	162	163	164
165	166	167	168	169	170	171
172	173	174	175	176	177	178
179	180	181	182	183	184	185
186	187	188	189	190	191	192
193	194	195	196	197	198	199
200	201	202	203	204	205	206

SURAH AL-A`RAF

JUZ #9 · SURAH #8

1	2	3	4	5	6	7
8	9	10	11	12	13	14
15	16	17	18	19	20	21
22	23	24	25	26	27	28
29	30	31	32	33	34	35
36	37	38	39	40		

SURAH AL-ANFAL

JUZ #10 · SURAH #8

41	42	43	44	45	46	47
48	49	50	51	52	53	54
55	56	57	58	59	60	61
62	63	64	65	66	67	68
69	70	71	72	73	74	75

SURAH AL-TAWBAH

JUZ #10 · SURAH #9

1	2	3	4	5	6	7
8	9	10	11	12	13	14
15	16	17	18	19	20	21
22	23	24	25	26	27	28
29	30	31	32	33	34	35
36	37	38	39	40	41	42
43	44	45	46	47	48	49
50	51	52	53	54	55	56
57	58	59	60	61	62	63
64	65	66	67	68	69	70

SURAH AL-TAWBAH

71	72	73	74	75	76	77
78	79	80	81	82	83	84
85	86	87	88	89	90	91
92						

SURAH AL-TAWBAH

						JUZ #11 • SURAH #9
93	94	95	96	97	98	99
100	101	102	103	104	105	106
107	108	109	110	111	112	113
114	115	116	117	118	119	120
121	122	123	124	125	126	127
128	129					

SURAH YUNUS

						JUZ #11 • SURAH #10
1	2	3	4	5	6	7
8	9	10	11	12	13	14
15	16	17	18	19	20	21
22	23	24	25	26	27	28
29	30	31	32	33	34	35
36	37	38	39	40	41	42
43	44	45	46	47	48	49
50	51	52	53	54	55	56
57	58	59	60	61	62	63

SURAH YUNUS

JUZ #11 • SURAH #10

64	65	66	67	68	69	70
71	72	73	74	75	76	77
78	79	80	81	82	83	84
85	86	87	88	89	90	91
92	93	94	95	96	97	98
99	100	101	102	103	104	105
106	107	108	109			

SURAH HUD

JUZ #11 • SURAH #11

1	2	3	4	5		

SURAH HUD

6	7	8	9	10	11	12
13	14	15	16	17	18	19
20	21	22	23	24	25	26
27	28	29	30	31	32	33
34	35	36	37	38	39	40
41	42	43	44	45	46	47
48	49	50	51	52	53	54
55	56	57	58	59	60	61
62	63	64	65	66	67	68
69	70	71	72	73	74	75
76	77	78	79	80	81	82
83	84	85	86	87	88	89
90	91	92	93	94	95	96
97	98	99	100	101	102	103
104	105	106	107	108	109	110
111	112	113	114	115	116	117
118	119	120	121	122	123	

SURAH YUSUF

JUZ #12 • SURAH #12

1	2	3	4	5	6	7
8	9	10	11	12	13	14
15	16	17	18	19	20	21
22	23	24	25	26	27	28
29	30	31	32	33	34	35
36	37	38	39	40	41	42
43	44	45	46	47	48	49
50	51	52				

SURAH YUSUF

JUZ #13 • SURAH #12

53	54	55	56	57	58	59
60	61	62	63	64	65	66
67	68	69	70	71	72	73
74	75	76	77	78	79	80
81	82	83	84	85	86	87
88	89	90	91	92	93	94
95	96	97	98	99	100	101
102	103	104	105	106	107	108
109	110	111				

SURAH AL-RA`D

JUZ #13 • SURAH #13

1	2	3	4	5	6	7
8	9	10	11	12	13	14
15	16	17	18	19	20	21
22	23	24	25	26	27	28
29	30	31	32	33	34	35
36	37	38	39	40	41	42
43						

SURAH IBRAHIM

JUZ #13 • SURAH #14

1	2	3	4	5	6	7
8	9	10	11	12	13	14
15	16	17	18	19	20	21
22	23	24	25	26	27	28
29	30	31	32	33	34	35
36	37	38	39	40	41	42
43	44	45	46	47	48	49
50	51	52				

SURAH AL-HIJR

JUZ #14 · SURAH #15

1	2	3	4	5	6	7
8	9	10	11	12	13	14
15	16	17	18	19	20	21
22	23	24	25	26	27	28
29	30	31	32	33	34	35
36	37	38	39	40	41	42
43	44	45	46	47	48	49
50	51	52	53	54	55	56
57	58	59	60	61	62	63
64	65	66	67	68	69	70
71	72	73	74	75	76	77
78	79	80	81	82	83	84
85	86	87	88	89	90	91
92	93	94	95	96	97	98
99						

SURAH AL-NAHL

JUZ #14 · SURAH #16

1	2	3	4	5	6	7
8	9	10	11	12	13	14
15	16	17	18	19	20	21
22	23	24	25	26	27	28
29	30	31	32	33	34	35
36	37	38	39	40	41	42
43	44	45	46	47	48	49
50	51	52	53	54	55	56
57	58	59	60	61	62	63
64	65	66	67	68	69	70
71	72	73	74	75	76	77
78	79	80	81	82	83	84
85	86	87	88	89	90	91
92	93	94	95	96	97	98
99	100	101	102	103	104	105
106	107	108	109	110	111	112
113	114	115	116	117	118	119

SURAH AL-NAHL

120	121	122	123	124	125	126
127	128					

SURAH AL-ISRA

1	2	3	4	5	6	7
8	9	10	11	12	13	14
15	16	17	18	19	20	21
22	23	24	25	26	27	28
29	30	31	32	33	34	35
36	37	38	39	40	41	42
43	44	45	46	47	48	49
50	51	52	53	54	55	56
57	58	59	60	61	62	63
64	65	66	67	68	69	70
71	72	73	74	75	76	77
78	79	80	81	82	83	84
85	86	87	88	89	90	91
92	93	94	95	96	97	98
99	100	101	102	103	104	105
106	107	108	109	110	111	

SURAH AL-KAHF

1	2	3	4	5	6	7
8	9	10	11	12	13	14
15	16	17	18	19	20	21
22	23	24	25	26	27	28
29	30	31	32	33	34	35
36	37	38	39	40	41	42
43	44	45	46	47	48	49
50	51	52	53	54	55	56
57	58	59	60	61	62	63
64	65	66	67	68	69	70
71	72	73	74			

SURAH AL-KAHF

JUZ #16 • SURAH #18

75	76	77	78	79	80	81
82	83	84	85	86	87	88
89	90	91	92	93	94	95
96	97	98	99	100	101	102
103	104	105	106	107	108	109
110						

SURAH MARYAM

JUZ #16 • SURAH #19

1	2	3	4	5	6	7
8	9	10	11	12	13	14
15	16	17	18	19	20	21
22	23	24	25	26	27	28
29	30	31	32	33	34	35
36	37	38	39	40	41	42
43	44	45	46	47	48	49
50	51	52	53	54	55	56
57	58	59	60	61	62	63

SURAH MARYAM

JUZ #16 • SURAH #19

64	65	66	67	68	69	70
71	72	73	74	75	76	77
78	79	80	81	82	83	84
85	86	87	88	89	90	91
92	93	94	95	96	97	98

SURAH TA-HA

JUZ #16 • SURAH #20

1	2	3	4	5	6	7
8	9	10	11	12	13	14
15	16	17	18	19	20	21
22	23	24	25	26	27	28
29	30	31	32	33	34	35
36	37	38	39	40	41	42
43	44	45	46	47	48	49
50	51	52	53	54	55	56
57	58	59	60	61	62	63
64	65	66	67	68	69	70

SURAH TA-HA

71	72	73	74	75	76	77
78	79	80	81	82	83	84
85	86	87	88	89	90	91
92	93	94	95	96	97	98
99	100	101	102	103	104	105
106	107	108	109	110	111	112
113	114	115	116	117	118	119
120	121	122	123	124	125	126
127	128	129	130	131	132	133
134	135					

SURAH AL-ANBIYA

JUZ #17 · SURAH #21

1	2	3	4	5	6	7
8	9	10	11	12	13	14
15	16	17	18	19	20	21
22	23	24	25	26	27	28
29	30	31	32	33	34	35
36	37	38	39	40	41	42
43	44	45	46	47	48	49
50	51	52	53	54	55	56
57	58	59	60	61	62	63
64	65	66	67	68	69	70
71	72	73	74	75	76	77
78	79	80	81	82	83	84
85	86	87	88	89	90	91
92	93	94	95	96	97	98
99	100	101	102	103	104	105
106	107	108	109	110	111	112

SURAH AL-HAJJ

1	2	3	4	5	6	7
8	9	10	11	12	13	14
15	16	17	18	19	20	21
22	23	24	25	26	27	28
29	30	31	32	33	34	35
36	37	38	39	40	41	42
43	44	45	46	47	48	49
50	51	52	53	54	55	56
57	58	59	60	61	62	63
64	65	66	67	68	69	70
71	72	73	74	75	76	77
78						

SURAH AL-MU'MINUN

JUZ #18 · SURAH #23

1	2	3	4	5	6	7
8	9	10	11	12	13	14
15	16	17	18	19	20	21
22	23	24	25	26	27	28
29	30	31	32	33	34	35
36	37	38	39	40	41	42
43	44	45	46	47	48	49
50	51	52	53	54	55	56
57	58	59	60	61	62	63
64	65	66	67	68	69	70
71	72	73	74	75	76	77
78	79	80	81	82	83	84
85	86	87	88	89	90	91
92	93	94	95	96	97	98
99	100	101	102	103	104	105
106	107	108	109	110	111	112
113	114	115	116	117	118	

SURAH AL-NUR

JUZ #18 · SURAH #24

1	2	3	4	5	6	7
8	9	10	11	12	13	14
15	16	17	18	19	20	21
22	23	24	25	26	27	28
29	30	31	32	33	34	35
36	37	38	39	40	41	42
43	44	45	46	47	48	49
50	51	52	53	54	55	56
57	58	59	60	61	62	63
64						

SURAH AL-FURQAN

JUZ #18 · SURAH #25

1	2	3	4	5	6	7
8	9	10	11	12	13	14
15	16	17	18	19	20	

SURAH AL-FURQAN

JUZ #19 • SURAH #25

21	22	23	24	25	26	27
28	29	30	31	32	33	34
35	36	37	38	39	40	41
42	43	44	45	46	47	48
49	50	51	52	53	54	55
56	57	58	59	60	61	62
63	64	65	66	67	68	69
70	71	72	73	74	75	76
77						

SURAH AL-SHU`ARA

JUZ #19 • SURAH #26

1	2	3	4	5	6	7
8	9	10	11	12	13	14
15	16	17	18	19	20	21
22	23	24	25	26	27	28
29	30	31	32	33	34	35
36	37	38	39	40	41	42

SURAH AL-SHU`ARA

JUZ #19 • SURAH #26

43	44	45	46	47	48	49
50	51	52	53	54	55	56
57	58	59	60	61	62	63
64	65	66	67	68	69	70
71	72	73	74	75	76	77
78	79	80	81	82	83	84
85	86	87	88	89	90	91
92	93	94	95	96	97	98
99	100	101	102	103	104	105
106	107	108	109	110	111	112
113	114	115	116	117	118	119
120	121	122	123	124	125	126
127	128	129	130	131	132	133
134	135	136	137	138	139	140
141	142	143	144	145	146	147
148	149	150	151	152	153	154
155	156	157	158	159	160	161

SURAH AL-SHU`ARA

JUZ #19 • SURAH #26

162	163	164	165	166	167	168
169	170	171	172	173	174	175
176	177	178	179	180	181	182
183	184	185	186	187	188	189
190	191	192	193	194	195	196
197	198	199	200	201	202	203
204	205	206	207	208	209	210
211	212	213	214	215	216	217
218	219	220	221	222	223	224
225	226	227				

SURAH AL-NAML

JUZ #19 • SURAH #27

1	2	3	4	5	6	7
8	9	10	11	12	13	14
15	16	17	18	19	20	21
22	23	24	25	26	27	28
36	37	38	39	40	41	42

SURAH AL-NAML

JUZ #19 • SURAH #27

43	44	45	46	47	48	49
50	51	52	53	54	55	

SURAH AL-NAML

JUZ #20 • SURAH #27

56	57	58	59	60	61	62
63	64	65	66	67	68	69
70	71	72	73	74	75	76
77	78	79	80	81	82	83
84	85	86	87	88	89	90
91	92	93				

SURAH AL-QASAS

JUZ #20 • SURAH #28

1	2	3	4	5	6	7
8	9	10	11	12	13	14
15	16	17	18	19	20	21
22	23	24	25	26	27	28
29	30	31	32	33	34	35
36	37	38	39	40	41	42
43	44	45	46	47	48	49
50	51	52	53	54	55	56
57	58	59	60	61	62	63

SURAH AL-QASAS

JUZ #20 • SURAH #28

64	65	66	67	68	69	70
71	72	73	74	75	76	77
78	79	80	81	82	83	84
85	86	87	88			

SURAH AL-`ANKABUT

JUZ #20 • SURAH #29

1	2	3	4	5	6	7
8	9	10	11	12	13	14
15	16	17	18	19	20	21
22	23	24	25	26	27	28
29	30	31	32	33	34	35
36	37	38	39	40	41	42
43	44	45				

SURAH AL-`ANKABUT

JUZ #21 • SURAH #29

46	47	48	49	50	51	52
53	54	55	56	57	58	59
60	61	62	63	64	65	66
67	68	69				

SURAH AL-RUM

JUZ #21 • SURAH #30

1	2	3	4	5	6	7
8	9	10	11	12	13	14
15	16	17	18	19	20	21
22	23	24	25	26	27	28
29	30	31	32	33	34	35
36	37	38	39	40	41	42
43	44	45	46	47	48	49
50	51	52	53	54	55	56
57	58	59	60			

SURAH LUQMAN

JUZ #21 · SURAH #31

1	2	3	4	5	6	7
8	9	10	11	12	13	14
15	16	17	18	19	20	21
22	23	24	25	26	27	28
29	30	31	32	33	34	

SURAH AL-SAJDAH

JUZ #21 · SURAH #32

1	2	3	4	5	6	7
8	9	10	11	12	13	14
15	16	17	18	19	20	21
22	23	24	25	26	27	28
29	30					

SURAH AL-AHZAB

JUZ #21 • SURAH #33

1	2	3	4	5	6	7
8	9	10	11	12	13	14
15	16	17	18	19	20	21
22	23	24	25	26	27	28
29	30					

SURAH AL-AHZAB

JUZ #22 • SURAH #33

31	32	33	34	35	36	37
38	39	40	41	42	43	44
45	46	47	48	49	50	51
52	53	54	55	56	57	58
59	60	61	62	63	64	65
66	67	68	69	70	71	72
73						

SURAH SABA

JUZ #22 • SURAH #34

1	2	3	4	5	6	7
8	9	10	11	12	13	14
15	16	17	18	19	20	21
22	23	24	25	26	27	28
29	30	31	32	33	34	35
36	37	38	39	40	41	42
43	44	45	46	47	48	49
50	51	52	53	54		

SURAH FATIR

1	2	3	4	5	6	7
8	9	10	11	12	13	14
15	16	17	18	19	20	21
22	23	24	25	26	27	28
29	30	31	32	33	34	35
36	37	38	39	40	41	42
43	44	45				

SURAH YA-SIN

1	2	3	4	5	6	7
8	9	10	11	12	13	14
15	16	17	18	19	20	21
22	23	24	25	26	27	

SURAH YA-SIN

JUZ #23 • SURAH #36

28	29	30	31	32	33	34
35	36	37	38	39	40	41
42	43	44	45	46	47	48
49	50	51	52	53	54	55
56	57	58	59	60	61	62
63	64	65	66	67	68	69
70	71	72	73	74	75	76
77	78	79	80	81	82	83

SURAH AL-SAFFAT

JUZ #23 • SURAH #37

1	2	3	4	5	6	7
8	9	10	11	12	13	14
15	16	17	18	19	20	21
22	23	24	25	26	27	28
29	30	31	32	33	34	35
36	37	38	39	40	41	42
43	44	45	46	47	48	49

SURAH AL-SAFFAT

50	51	52	53	54	55	56
57	58	59	60	61	62	63
64	65	66	67	68	69	70
71	72	73	74	75	76	77
78	79	80	81	82	83	84
85	86	87	88	89	90	91
92	93	94	95	96	97	98
99	100	101	102	103	104	105
106	107	108	109	110	111	112
113	114	115	116	117	118	119
120	121	122	123	124	125	126
127	128	129	130	131	132	133
134	135	136	137	138	139	140
141	142	143	144	145	146	147
148	149	150	151	152	153	154
155	156	157	158	159	160	161
162	163	164	165	166	167	168

SURAH AL-SAFFAT

JUZ #23 • SURAH #37

169	170	171	172	173	174	175
176	177	178	179	180	181	182

SURAH SAD

JUZ #23 • SURAH #38

1	2	3	4	5	6	7
8	9	10	11	12	13	14
15	16	17	18	19	20	21
22	23	24	25	26	27	28
29	30	31	32	33	34	35
36	37	38	39	40	41	42
43	44	45	46	47	48	49
50	51	52	53	54	55	56
57	58	59	60	61	62	63
64	65	66	67	68	69	70
71	72	73	74	75	76	77
78	79	80	81	82	83	84
85	86	87	88			

SURAH AL-ZUMAR

JUZ #23 · SURAH #39

1	2	3	4	5	6	7
8	9	10	11	12	13	14
15	16	17	18	19	20	21
22	23	24	25	26	27	28
29	30	31				

SURAH AL-ZUMAR

JUZ #24 • SURAH #39

32	33	34	35	36	37	38
39	40	41	42	43	44	45
46	47	48	49	50	51	52
53	54	55	56	57	58	59
60	61	62	63	64	65	66
67	68	69	70	71	72	73
74	75					

SURAH GHAFIR

JUZ #24 • SURAH #40

1	2	3	4	5	6	7
8	9	10	11	12	13	14
15	16	17	18	19	20	21
22	23	24	25	26	27	28
29	30	31	32	33	34	35
36	37	38	39	40	41	42
43	44	45	46	47	48	49
50	51	52	53	54	55	56

SURAH GHAFIR

JUZ #24 • SURAH #40

57	58	59	60	61	62	63
64	65	66	67	68	69	70
71	72	73	74	75	76	77
78	79	80	81	82	83	84
85						

SURAH FUSSILAT

JUZ #24 • SURAH #41

1	2	3	4	5	6	7
8	9	10	11	12	13	14
15	16	17	18	19	20	21
22	23	24	25	26	27	28
29	30	31	32	33	34	35
36	37	38	39	40	41	42
43	44	45	46			

SURAH FUSSILAT

JUZ #25 • SURAH #41

47	48	49	50	51	52	53
54						

SURAH AL-SHURA

JUZ #25 • SURAH #42

1	2	3	4	5	6	7
8	9	10	11	12	13	14
15	16	17	18	19	20	21
22	23	24	25	26	27	28
29	30	31	32	33	34	35
36	37	38	39	40	41	42
43	44	45	46	47	48	49
50	51	52	53			

SURAH AL-ZUKHRUF

JUZ #25 • SURAH #43

1	2	3	4	5	6	7
8	9	10	11	12	13	14
15	16	17	18	19	20	21

SURAH AL-ZUKHRUF

JUZ #25 • SURAH #43

21	22	23	24	25	26	27
28	29	30	31	32	33	34
35	36	37	38	39	40	41
42	43	44	45	46	47	48
49	50	51	52	53	54	55
56	57	58	59	60	61	62
63	64	65	66	67	68	69
70	71	72	73	74	75	76
77	78	79	80	81	82	83
84	85	86	87	88	89	

SURAH AL-DUKHAN

JUZ #25 • SURAH #44

1	2	3	4	5	6	7
8	9	10	11	12	13	14
15	16	17	18	19	20	21
22	23	24	25	26	27	28
29	30	31	32	33	34	35

SURAH AL-DUKHAN

JUZ #25 • SURAH #44

36	37	38	39	40	41	42
43	44	45	46	47	48	49
50	51	52	53	54	55	56
57	58	59				

SURAH AL-JATHIYAH

JUZ #25 • SURAH #45

1	2	3	4	5	6	7
8	9	10	11	12	13	14
15	16	17	18	19	20	21
22	23	24	25	26	27	28
29	30	31	32	33	34	35
36	37					

SURAH AL-AHQAF

JUZ #26 · SURAH #46

1	2	3	4	5	6	7
8	9	10	11	12	13	14
15	16	17	18	19	20	21
22	23	24	25	26	27	28
29	30	31	32	33	34	35

SURAH MUHAMMAD

JUZ #26 · SURAH #47

1	2	3	4	5	6	7
8	9	10	11	12	13	14
15	16	17	18	19	20	21
22	23	24	25	26	27	28
29	30	31	32	33	34	35
36	37	38				

SURAH AL-FATH

JUZ #26 • SURAH #48

1	2	3	4	5	6	7
8	9	10	11	12	13	14
15	16	17	18	19	20	21
22	23	24	25	26	27	28
29						

SURAH AL-HUJURAT

JUZ #26 • SURAH #49

1	2	3	4	5	6	7
8	9	10	11	12	13	14
15	16	17	18			

SURAH QAF

JUZ #26 • SURAH #50

1	2	3	4	5	6	7
8	9	10	11	12	13	14
15	16	17	18	19	20	21
22	23	24	25	26	27	28
29	30	31	32	33	34	35

PROGRESS TRACKER

SURAH QAF

JUZ #26 · SURAH #50

36	37	38	39	40	41	42
43	44	45				

SURAH AL-DHARIYAT

JUZ #26 · SURAH #51

1	2	3	4	5	6	7
8	9	10	11	12	13	14
15	16	17	18	19	20	21
22	23	24	25	26	27	28
29	30					

133

SURAH AL-DHARIYAT

JUZ #27 • SURAH #51

31	32	33	34	35	36	37
38	39	40	41	42	43	44
45	46	47	48	49	50	51
52	53	54	55	56	57	58
59	60					

SURAH AL-TUR

JUZ #27 • SURAH #52

1	2	3	4	5	6	7
8	9	10	11	12	13	14
15	16	17	18	19	20	21
22	23	24	25	26	27	28
29	30	31	32	33	34	35
36	37	38	39	40	41	42
43	44	45	46	47	48	49

SURAH AL-NAJM

JUZ #27 • SURAH #53

1	2	3	4	5	6	7
8	9	10	11	12	13	14
15	16	17	18	19	20	21
22	23	24	25	26	27	28
29	30	31	32	33	34	35
36	37	38	39	40	41	42
43	44	45	46	47	48	49
50	51	52	53	54	55	56
57	58	59	60	61	62	

SURAH AL-QAMAR

JUZ #27 • SURAH #54

1	2	3	4	5	6	7
8	9	10	11	12	13	14
15	16	17	18	19	20	21
22	23	24	25	26	27	28
29	30	31	32	33	34	35
36	37	38	39	40	41	42

SURAH AL-QAMAR

43	44	45	46	47	48	49
50	51	52	53	54	55	

SURAH AL-RAHMAN

1	2	3	4	5	6	7
8	9	10	11	12	13	14
15	16	17	18	19	20	21
22	23	24	25	26	27	28
29	30	31	32	33	34	35
36	37	38	39	40	41	42
43	44	45	46	47	48	49
50	51	52	53	54	55	56
57	58	59	60	61	62	63
64	65	66	67	68	69	70
71	72	73	74	75	76	77
78						

SURAH AL-WAQI`AH

1	2	3	4	5	6	7
8	9	10	11	12	13	14
15	16	17	18	19	20	21
22	23	24	25	26	27	28
29	30	31	32	33	34	35
36	37	38	39	40	41	42
43	44	45	46	47	48	49
50	51	52	53	54	55	56
57	58	59	60	61	62	63
64	65	66	67	68	69	70
71	72	73	74	75	76	77
78	79	80	81	82	83	84
85	86	87	88	89	90	91
92	93	94	95	96		

SURAH AL-HADID

1	2	3	4	5	6	7
8	9	10	11	12	13	14
15	16	17	18	19	20	21
22	23	24	25	26	27	28
29						

SURAH AL-MUJADILAH

JUZ #28 • SURAH #58

1	2	3	4	5	6	7
8	9	10	11	12	13	14
15	16	17	18	19	20	21
22						

SURAH AL-HASHR

JUZ #28 • SURAH #59

1	2	3	4	5	6	7
8	9	10	11	12	13	14
15	16	17	18	19	20	21
22	23	24				

SURAH AL-MUMTAHANAH

JUZ #28 • SURAH #60

1	2	3	4	5	6	7
8	9	10	11	12	13	

SURAH AL-SAF

JUZ #28 • SURAH #61

1	2	3	4	5	6	7
8	9	10	11	12	13	14

PROGRESS TRACKER

SURAH AL-JUMU`AH

JUZ #28 • SURAH #62

1	2	3	4	5	6	7
8	9	10	11			

SURAH AL-MUNAFIQUN

JUZ #28 • SURAH #63

1	2	3	4	5	6	7
8	9	10	11			

SURAH AL-TAGHABUN

JUZ #28 • SURAH #64

1	2	3	4	5	6	7
8	9	10	11	12	13	14
15	16	17	18			

SURAH AL-TALAQ

JUZ #28 • SURAH #65

1	2	3	4	5	6	7
8	9	10	11	12		

SURAH AL-TAHRIM

JUZ #28 · SURAH #66

1	2	3	4	5	6	7
8	9	10	11	12		

SURAH AL-MULK

JUZ #29 • SURAH #67

1	2	3	4	5	6	7
8	9	10	11	12	13	14
15	16	17	18	19	20	21
22	23	24	25	26	27	28
29	30					

SURAH AL-QALAM

JUZ #29 • SURAH #68

1	2	3	4	5	6	7
8	9	10	11	12	13	14
15	16	17	18	19	20	21
22	23	24	25	26	27	28
29	30	31	32	33	34	35
36	37	38	39	40	41	42
43	44	45	46	47	48	49
50	51	52				

SURAH AL-HAQQAH

JUZ #29 • SURAH #69

1	2	3	4	5	6	7
8	9	10	11	12	13	14
15	16	17	18	19	20	21
22	23	24	25	26	27	28
29	30	31	32	33	34	35
36	37	38	39	40	41	42
43	44	45	46	47	48	49
50	51	52				

SURAH AL-MA`ARIJ

JUZ #29 • SURAH #70

1	2	3	4	5	6	7
8	9	10	11	12	13	14
15	16	17	18	19	20	21
22	23	24	25	26	27	28
29	30	31	32	33	34	35
36	37	38	39	40	41	42
43	44					

SURAH NUH

JUZ #29 • SURAH #71

1	2	3	4	5	6	7
8	9	10	11	12	13	14
15	16	17	18	19	20	21
22	23	24	25	26	27	28

SURAH AL-JINN

JUZ #29 • SURAH #72

1	2	3	4	5	6	7
8	9	10	11	12	13	14
15	16	17	18	19	20	21
22	23	24	25	26	27	28

SURAH AL-MUZZAMMIL

JUZ #29 • SURAH #73

1	2	3	4	5	6	7
8	9	10	11	12	13	14
15	16	17	18	19	20	

SURAH AL-MUDDATHTHIR

JUZ #29 • SURAH #74

1	2	3	4	5	6	7
8	9	10	11	12	13	14
15	16	17	18	19	20	21
22	23	24	25	26	27	28
29	30	31	32	33	34	35
36	37	38	39	40	41	42
43	44	45	46	47	48	49
50	51	52	53	54	55	56

SURAH AL-QIYAMAH

JUZ #29 • SURAH #75

1	2	3	4	5	6	7
8	9	10	11	12	13	14
15	16	17	18	19	20	21
22	23	24	25	26	27	28
29	30	31	32	33	34	35
36	37	38	39	40		

SURAH AL-INSAN

JUZ #29 • SURAH #76

1	2	3	4	5	6	7
8	9	10	11	12	13	14
15	16	17	18	19	20	21
22	23	24	25	26	27	28
29	30	31				

SURAH AL-MURSALAT

JUZ #29 • SURAH #77

1	2	3	4	5	6	7
8	9	10	11	12	13	14
15	16	17	18	19	20	21
22	23	24	25	26	27	28
29	30	31	32	33	34	35
36	37	38	39	40	41	42
43	44	45	46	47	48	49
50						

SURAH AL-NABA

JUZ #30 · SURAH #78

1	2	3	4	5	6	7
8	9	10	11	12	13	14
15	16	17	18	19	20	21
22	23	24	25	26	27	28
29	30	31	32	33	34	35
36	37	38	39	40		

SURAH AL-NAZI`AT

JUZ #30 · SURAH #79

1	2	3	4	5	6	7
8	9	10	11	12	13	14
15	16	17	18	19	20	21
22	23	24	25	26	27	28
29	30	31	32	33	34	35
36	37	38	39	40	41	42
43	44	45	46			

SURAH `ABASA

JUZ #30 · SURAH #80

1	2	3	4	5	6	7
8	9	10	11	12	13	14
15	16	17	18	19	20	21
22	23	24	25	26	27	28
29	30	31	32	33	34	35
36	37	38	39	40	41	42

SURAH AL-TAKWIR

JUZ #30 · SURAH #81

1	2	3	4	5	6	7
8	9	10	11	12	13	14
15	16	17	18	19	20	21
22	23	24	25	26	27	28
29						

SURAH AL-INFITAR

JUZ #30 • SURAH #82

1	2	3	4	5	6	7
8	9	10	11	12	13	14
15	16	17	18	19		

SURAH AL-MUTAFFIFIN

JUZ #30 • SURAH #83

1	2	3	4	5	6	7
8	9	10	11	12	13	14
15	16	17	18	19	20	21
22	23	24	25	26	27	28
29	30	31	32	33	34	35
36						

SURAH AL-INSHIQAQ

JUZ #30 • SURAH #84

1	2	3	4	5	6	7
8	9	10	11	12	13	14
15	16	17	18	19	20	21
22	23	24	25			

SURAH AL-BURUJ

1	2	3	4	5	6	7
8	9	10	11	12	13	14
15	16	17	18	19	20	21
22						

SURAH AL-TARIQ

1	2	3	4	5	6	7
8	9	10	11	12	13	14
15	16	17				

SURAH AL-A`LA

1	2	3	4	5	6	7
8	9	10	11	12	13	14
15	16	17	18	19		

SURAH AL-GHASHIYAH

JUZ #30 • SURAH #88

1	2	3	4	5	6	7
8	9	10	11	12	13	14
15	16	17	18	19	20	21
22	23	24	25	26		

SURAH AL-FAJR

JUZ #30 • SURAH #89

1	2	3	4	5	6	7
8	9	10	11	12	13	14
15	16	17	18	19	20	21
22	23	24	25	26	27	28
29	30					

SURAH AL-BALAD

JUZ #30 • SURAH #90

1	2	3	4	5	6	7
8	9	10	11	12	13	14
15	16	17	18	19	20	

SURAH AL-SHAMS

JUZ #30 • SURAH #91

1	2	3	4	5	6	7
8	9	10	11	12	13	14
15						

SURAH AL-LAYL

JUZ #30 • SURAH #92

1	2	3	4	5	6	7
8	9	10	11	12	13	14
15	16	17	18	19	20	21

SURAH AD-DUHA

JUZ #30 • SURAH #93

1	2	3	4	5	6	7
8	9	10	11			

SURAH AL-SHARH

JUZ #30 • SURAH #94

1	2	3	4	5	6	7
8						

PROGRESS TRACKER

SURAH AL-TIN

JUZ #30 • SURAH #95

1	2	3	4	5	6	7
8						

SURAH AL-`ALAQ

JUZ #30 • SURAH #96

1	2	3	4	5	6	7
8	9	10	11	12	13	14
15	16	17	18	19		

SURAH AL-QADR

JUZ #30 • SURAH #97

1	2	3	4	5		

SURAH AL-BAYYINAH

JUZ #30 • SURAH #98

1	2	3	4	5	6	7
8						

SURAH AZ-ZALZALAH

JUZ #30 • SURAH #99

1	2	3	4	5	6	7
8						

SURAH AL-`ADIYAT

JUZ #30 • SURAH #100

1	2	3	4	5	6	7
8	9	10	11			

SURAH AL-QARI`AH

JUZ #30 • SURAH #101

1	2	3	4	5	6	7
8	9	10	11			

SURAH AL-TAKATHUR

JUZ #30 • SURAH #102

1	2	3	4	5	6	7
8						

SURAH AL-`ASR

JUZ #30 • SURAH #103

1	2	3

SURAH AL-HUMAZAH

JUZ #30 • SURAH #104

1	2	3	4	5	6	7
8	9					

PROGRESS TRACKER

SURAH AL-FIL
JUZ #30 • SURAH #105

1	2	3	4	5		

SURAH QURAYSH
JUZ #30 • SURAH #106

1	2	3	4			

SURAH AL-MA`UN
JUZ #30 • SURAH #107

1	2	3	4	5	6	7

SURAH AL-KAWTHAR
JUZ #30 • SURAH #108

1	2	3				

SURAH AL-KAFIRUN
JUZ #30 • SURAH #109

1	2	3	4	5	6	

SURAH AL-NASR
JUZ #30 • SURAH #110

1	2	3				

SURAH AL-MASAD
JUZ #30 • SURAH #111

1	2	3	4	5		

SURAH AL-IKHLAS

JUZ #30 • SURAH #112

1	2	3	4			

SURAH AL-FALAQ

JUZ #30 • SURAH #113

1	2	3	4	5		

SURAH AL-NAS

JUZ #30 • SURAH #114

1	2	3	4	5	6	

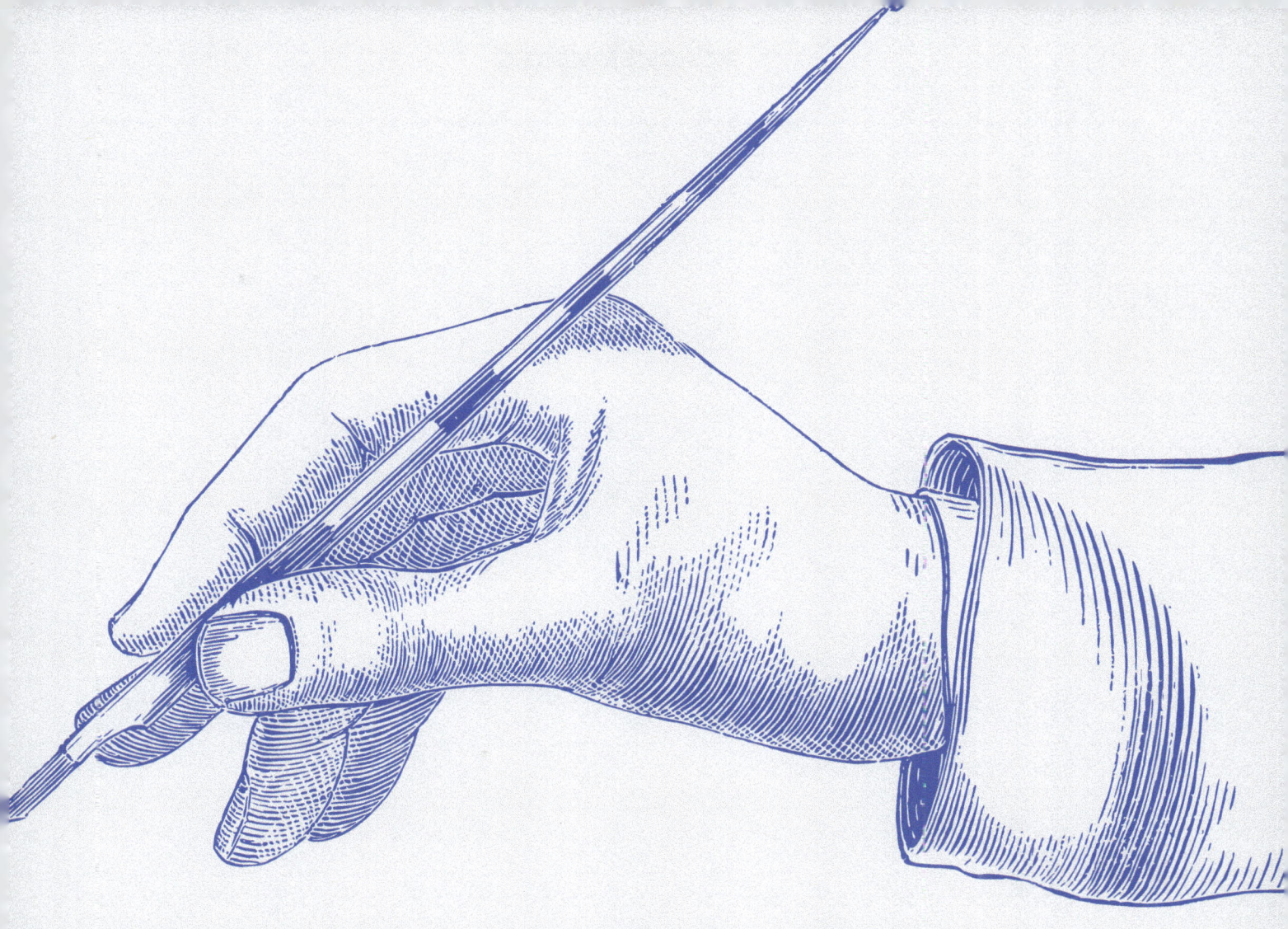

TEACHER NOTES

TEACHER NOTES